BEGINNING SCIENCE
WITH MR. WIZARD

BEGINNING SCIENCE
WITH MR. WIZARD

LIGHT

Don Herbert and Hy Ruchlis

ILLUSTRATED BY MEL HUNTER

DOUBLEDAY & COMPANY, INC.
GARDEN CITY, NEW YORK
1960

Have you ever seen a solid thing that sometimes can be completely invisible? You see such a thing every day in the week! Yet you pay no attention to it at all.

Look through a window at night while standing outside in the dark. Look for the glass. You know it's there. You can feel it if you reach out. Yet you can't see the glass at all.

Now look at a window of a dark room from the outside. You can't see a thing inside. But you will notice the glass now, because there are the reflections on it from lights in the street.

Why does this happen?

When light hits glass, several things take place. A small part of the light is reflected (bounces back). But most of the light passes right through the transparent glass.

When you stand in the dark outside the lighted room, reflection of light from the glass window to your eyes is very weak, as compared with the light coming straight through from in the room. So you see the inside of the room, but you do not see the glass at all!

This experiment shows that light must reach your eyes in order for you to see anything. If light is not reflected from the object to your eyes, and if it does not give off its own light, then you cannot see it. It is invisible.

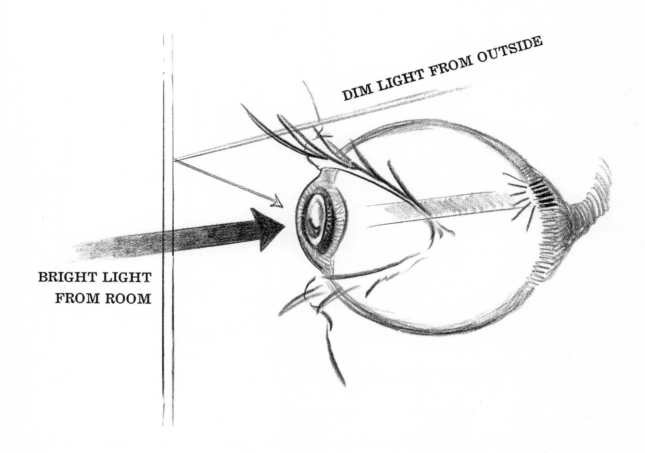

DIM LIGHT FROM OUTSIDE

BRIGHT LIGHT
FROM ROOM

Put a penny into a cup that is not made of transparent glass. Move away from the cup, and down, until the edge of the cup blocks the penny from sight. Now slowly pour water into the cup without moving your head. The penny gradually comes back into view!

Before you add water, the light that is reflected from the penny and travels toward your eyes doesn't reach you because the material of the cup stops it. Such a material is called "opaque."

When you add water, light from the penny bends and gets around the edge of the cup to your eye. So the penny is now visible.

Now do a similar experiment with a glass of water. Hold it up and look through it at some bright object. Everything appears wavy, broken, and out of shape. Light rays from the object are bent by the glass and the water in it.

All transparent materials can bend light in this way. This bending of light is called "refraction."

Now let's send some beams of light through a jar of water and see the way in which they bend. Set up a flashlight, a card with several vertical (top-to-bottom) slits, and a jar of water on a piece of white paper, like this.

An easy way to make the slits is to cut several four-inch lengths of card, about three quarters of an inch wide, and then use gummed tape to fasten the tops and bottoms together, with a slight space between strips. By bending the card at each side you can stand it on edge.

Point the flashlight slightly downward so that you see the beams of light on the paper. Look down from above. This is what you see.

Add a small amount of soap to the water. The increased reflection of light from the soap particles makes the beam more visible.

Notice how the water in the jar bends the rays of light from the flashlight so that they come together at one point. This is how you focus rays of light.

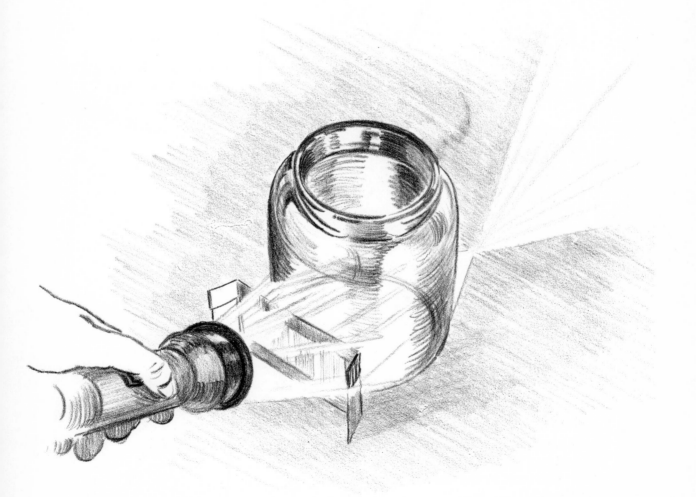

Place a pencil in water in a glass jar. In certain positions the pencil looks as though it were broken in two.

Look through a bottle of water at a ruler. The bottle acts as a magnifying glass and makes a bigger image.

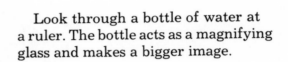

A clear glass marble acts as a lens. Hold it up very close to a wall and note the tiny image that is formed on the wall.

Move your head to one side as you look out of a window. Uneven spots in the glass show up as wavy appearance of distant objects. This effect is caused by refraction.

Put the point of a pencil just beneath the surface of water in a glass and view it from below. You see a mirror image of the point, while the pencil above the water is not seen at all.

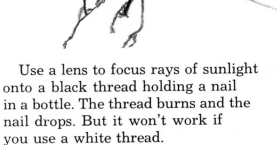

Use a lens to focus rays of sunlight onto a black thread holding a nail in a bottle. The thread burns and the nail drops. But it won't work if you use a white thread.

Now try this experiment. On a sunny day, outdoors, move a magnifying glass to and from a sheet of paper put in a sunny spot. At a certain position the rays of sunlight focus to a point.

Let the rays focus on a dark spot on the paper. An ink spot will do. The black surface of the ink spot absorbs (takes in) the rays of the sun, rather than reflecting them away. The paper gets hotter, soon begins to smoke, and may even catch fire. If this should happen, be ready to put it out quickly.

Stir up some dust in the path of the light passing through the lens. Dust particles reflect some of the sunlight to your eye so that you will be able to see the beam.

The lens and the jar of water focus rays of light in a similar way. But the lens does a much better job, because it has been specially shaped to focus light to a sharper point.

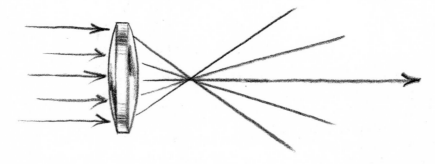

Hold up a magnifying glass near a wall opposite a window and move it back and forth. When the lens is at the right distance from the wall you see an image of the window on the wall. If a friend walks past the window you see a small picture of him "walking" upside down on the wall! In fact, you can see images of houses, trees, cars, and other things, all upside down (inverted).

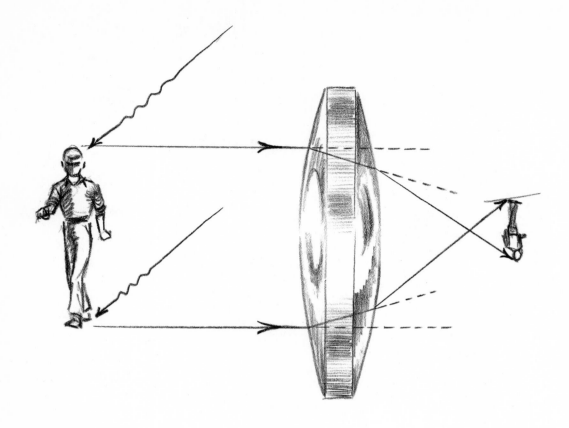

Here's why you can see the inverted image of your friend. Suppose that your friend is standing in sunlight in front of your lens. Light from the sun strikes his head and bounces off. Some of it reaches your lens and passes through. The lens bends the rays and brings them to a focus on the wall, like this.

Some of the rays of sunlight strike his feet and are reflected toward the lens. They pass through the lens and are brought to a focus like this.

Notice how rays from his head focus on the lower part of the wall. As a result an inverted image is formed.

Lenses are used in cameras to form images. The lens is at the front of a camera and produces an image on the film at the back. Chemicals on the film change when they are hit by light. This change remains on the film for a long time. When the film is developed, the chemical changes show up as dark or clear areas. The image is thereby captured on the film.

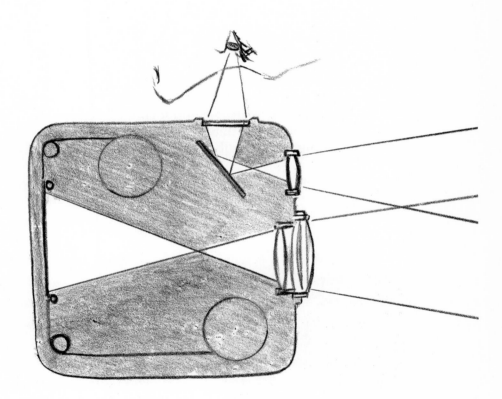

When you look at a fish tank from one corner you can see one fish appear as two. Both sides of the tank create different bending angles, causing a double image.

Hold a hand magnifying glass above the bulb of a table lamp. The lens acts as a projector and forms a greatly enlarged image of the markings of the bulb on the ceiling.

The bottoms of thick drinking glasses are often concave (curve inward). Look through the bottom of such a glass and note that everything appears right-side up and smaller.

Make a wave in a large flat pan with water in it. Push the water with a ruler or wide piece of cardboard. A wave travels outward and reflects off the side of the pan. A light wave is reflected in a similar manner.

While riding in a car on a sunny day watch for "mirages." Pools of water appear in the road ahead and disappear as you approach them. This "optical illusion" is caused by the bending of light rays by warm air near the ground. The "pools" look like water because they give a bright reflection of the sky, like real water does. Look for upside-down images of cars in these false pools of water.

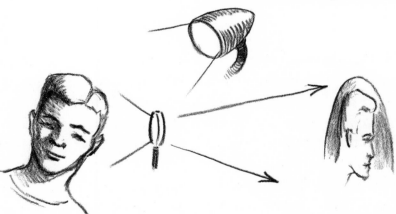

You may be able to project an enlarged image of a person on a wall by shining a strong light at his face and placing a lens nearby. Move the lens back and forth until the image is in focus on a wall.

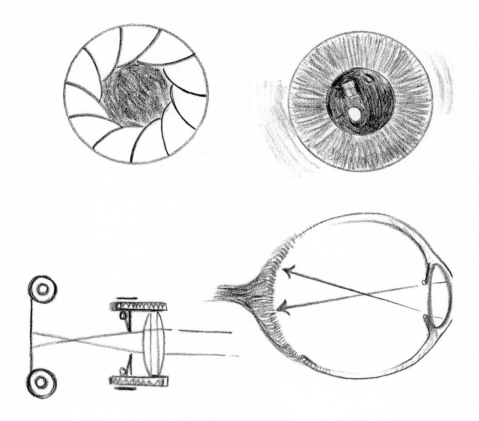

Walk into any room and look around. It is certain that there are a couple of lenses around. Where? Right in your eyes!

Each one of your eyes is like a small camera. A transparent bulging part near the front of the eyeball serves as a lens. It forms an image on the retina, a special layer of tissue at the back of the eyeball.

When the light reaches the thousands upon thousands of nerves in the retina, electric currents race up the nerves to your brain. These electrical messages form a pattern that the brain "reads" to tell you what kind of image is on the retina and, therefore, what kind of object you are looking at.

But just a moment. The image in your eye is upside down! Then why do you see things right-side up?

Your brain learns by experience what the different messages of electric current from your retina mean. When you were a few days old you saw nothing but light and dark, without any meaning at all. You gradually learned to connect certain patterns of light and dark with certain objects in their right positions. After a while you could "see" the objects and recognize what they were.

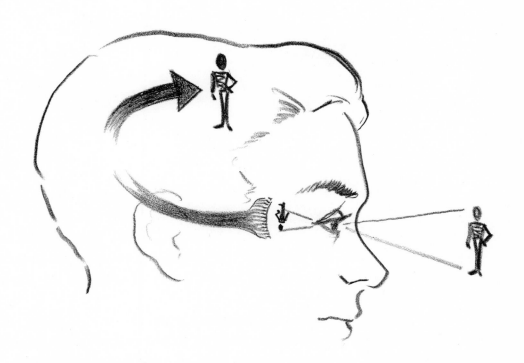

While studying about light, scientists have found many ways to help you see things more clearly. For example, a magnifying glass helps you to see tiny objects better. It is so simple that you can actually make one out of water!

Simply put a piece of wax paper on a newspaper and place a drop of water on the wax paper. The newspaper print appears greatly magnified. Try this with a drop of glycerine. It works even better.

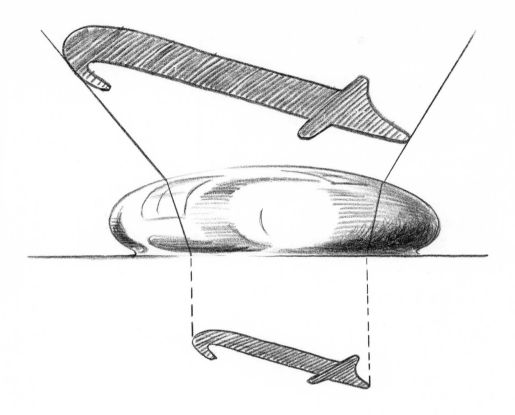

Why does this drop magnify? It has a bulging shape. Such a shape is called "convex." A magnifying glass also has this bulging shape. Suppose that you are looking at the letter "t" on a newspaper through a bulging drop of water or a lens. Light rays from the top and bottom of the "t" are bent by such a convex lens in the following way.

As a result you think that the light from the top of the "t" came from a point higher than it really did. At the same time you think that light from the bottom of the "t" came from a point lower than it really did. So the image that you see widens out and looks much bigger than it really is.

Like a good scientist, you should have been wondering why light bends when it passes through a transparent material.

Scientists have discovered that in some ways light acts as a wave. The speed of this wave in air and in space is about 186,000 miles a second, fast enough to go around the earth in the time it takes to wink your eye! It takes about eight minutes for light to reach the earth from the sun.

But light waves slow down as they travel from air into materials such as water and glass. If one part of the wave strikes the surface first, it slows down, while the other part is still traveling at its normal speed in the air. So the whole wave swings around and changes its direction.

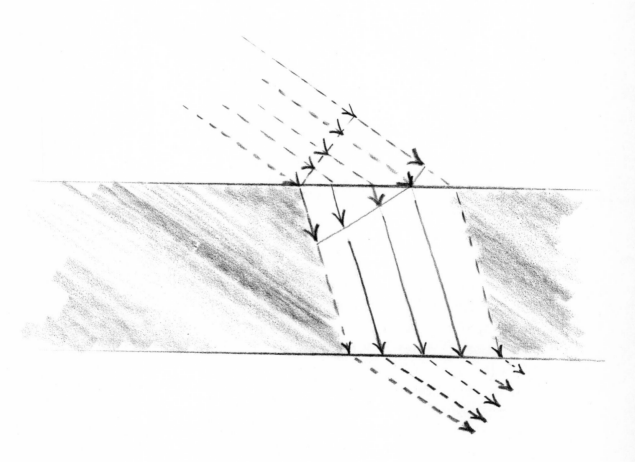

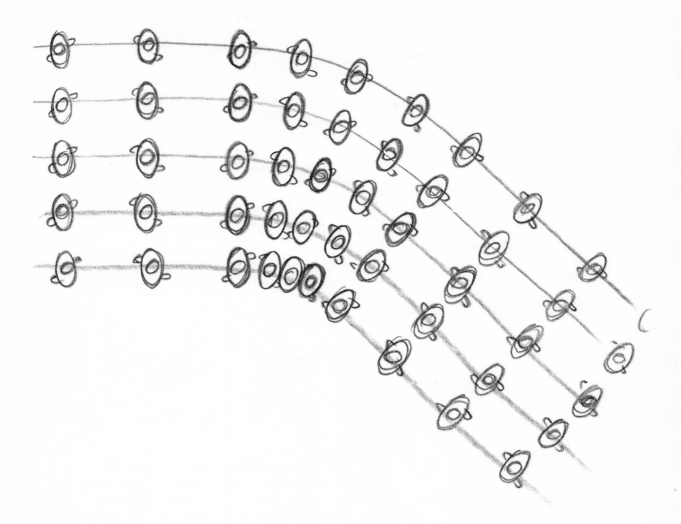

You might compare this moving wave with a line of marching soldiers in a parade. If the marchers on one side of the line slow down, the other side of the line swings around. The whole line then changes its direction. In fact, that is exactly how a line in a parade goes around a corner.

Without this simple slowing down of a light wave in a transparent material, lenses would not form images, and we could not see as well as we do.

Look through the lenses of a pair of eyeglasses held at arm's length. If the wearer of the glasses is farsighted you will probably see upside-down images in his convex lenses. If he is nearsighted you will see small upright images in his concave lenses.

Watch the streamers of light that form on the bottom of a shallow stream or pond while the sun is shining overhead. They are caused by the curved surface of the wavy water on top of the stream, which refracts the light as a lens does.

The shadow of a water bug that walks on the surface of water appears on the bottom of a shallow stream with large dark ovals around each leg. These dark areas are caused by the fact that the water is depressed under each leg by the weight of the bug and forms a concave "lens" of water. This concave shape then bends light away from the area and causes the large dark oval.

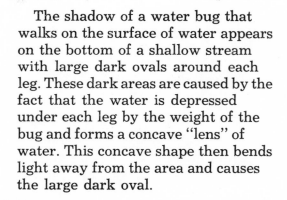

26

Use a round fish bowl filled with water as a lens to focus rays of light onto a piece of paper. You may also be able to form an image of the window with it.

Watch the sun as it goes down below the horizon at sunset. Notice how it appears flattened. This effect is caused by the bending of light from the sun as it passes from outer space through the air near the earth. The day is actually lengthened a few minutes each day because of this refraction of light.

Make a simple telescope by placing a concave lens near your eye and a convex lens beyond it. Move the convex lens toward and away from the concave lens until you see a magnified image.

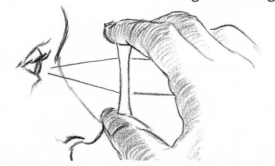

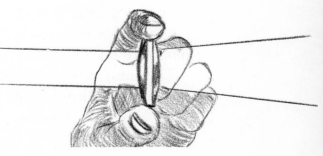

Our knowledge of light has enabled us to make eyeglasses, telescopes, microscopes, projectors, and cameras. These instruments make your life healthier and happier and add much to our knowledge of the world. How do such devices work?

The drawing shows how light is bent by the lenses of eyeglasses. Suppose that there is something wrong with the lenses of a person's eyes and these do not bring the rays from the letters in a book to focus on the retina. The first diagram shows how the rays travel without glasses. Notice how the rays cross instead of meeting on the retina. As a result the image is blurred. The person does not see clearly.

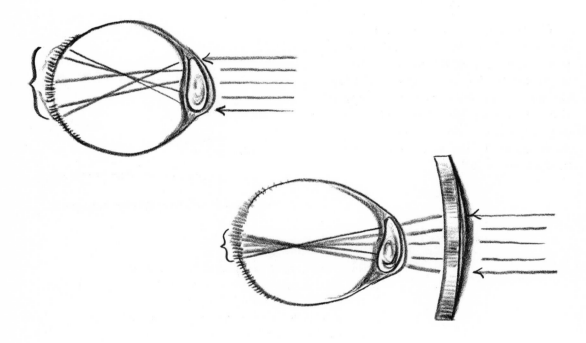

In the second diagram, notice how a special lens, just right for that person, spreads the rays apart and makes the rays come to a focus on the retina. Now the person sees clearly.

Different lenses are used for different people. The optometrist measures the kind of lens that is just right for each person.

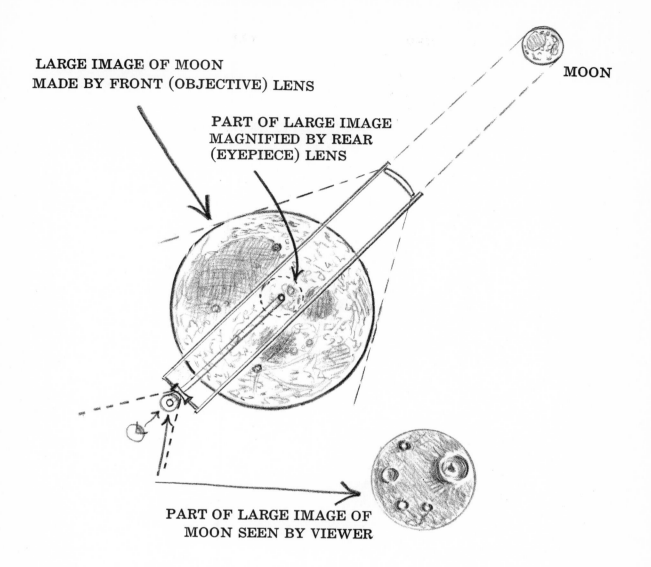

LARGE IMAGE OF MOON
MADE BY FRONT (OBJECTIVE) LENS

PART OF LARGE IMAGE
MAGNIFIED BY REAR
(EYEPIECE) LENS

MOON

PART OF LARGE IMAGE OF
MOON SEEN BY VIEWER

With telescopes man has been able to see about a billion light-years out into space. A light-year is the distance light travels in one year—at a speed of 186,000 miles each second!

Small telescopes usually have two or three lenses. The front lens forms a magnified image, which is then further magnified by the lens near your eye.

Try looking at the moon with a simple telescope or field glasses, and you will get some of the thrill that astronomers get with their big telescopes.

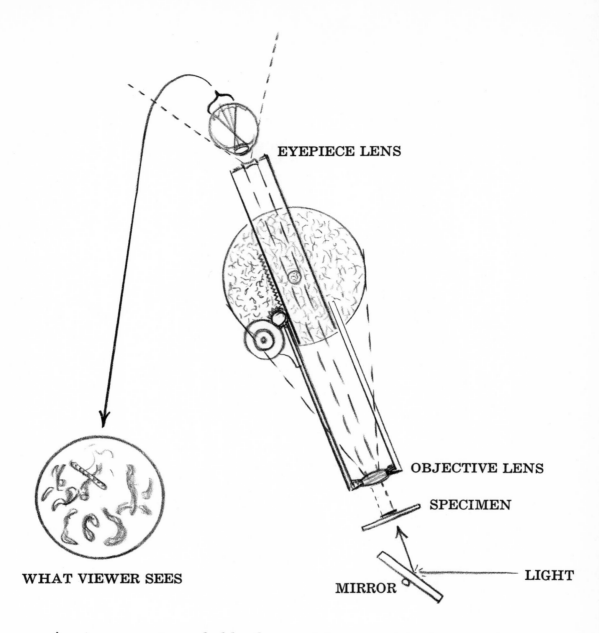

EYEPIECE LENS

OBJECTIVE LENS

SPECIMEN

LIGHT

MIRROR

WHAT VIEWER SEES

A microscope is probably the most important instrument in all of science. Here is how it works.

The main lens, at the bottom of the microscope tube, forms a magnified image near the top of the tube. The eyepiece then magnifies this image still more.

A great deal of light is needed because of the high magnification. Therefore, a microscope has a mirror under the slide to reflect light up into the lens.

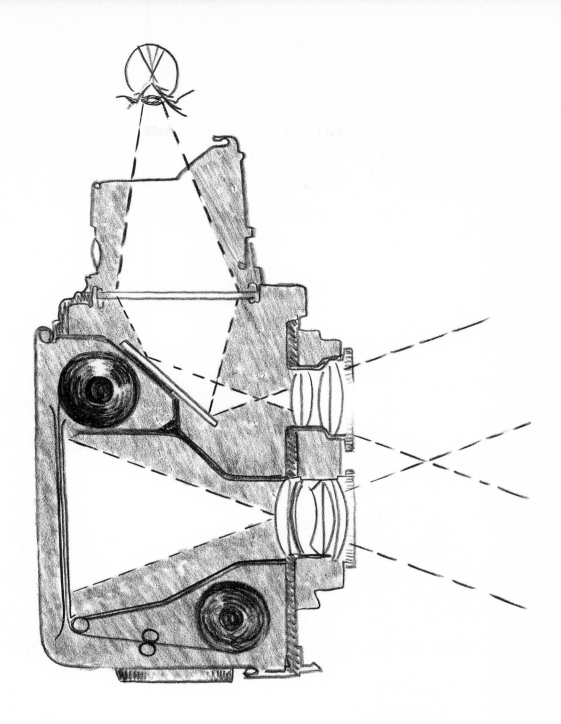

Here is a camera in more detail than you saw earlier. In this particular kind of camera there is a separate set of lenses, so that you can see the image on a ground glass that is very nearly like the image that is going to be focused on the film.

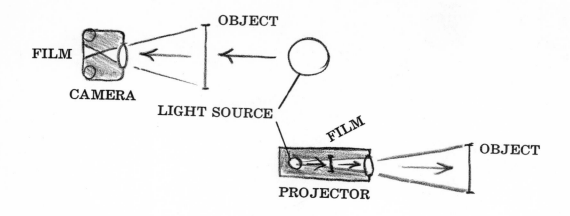

FILM
CAMERA
OBJECT
LIGHT SOURCE
FILM
PROJECTOR
OBJECT

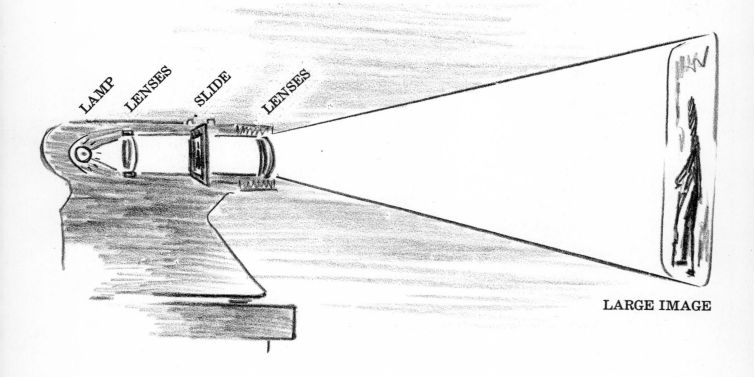

LAMP　LENSES　SLIDE　LENSES

LARGE IMAGE

You have often seen a projector which enlarges color slides made with a still or motion-picture camera. A beam of light goes through the slide, and a big image of it is flashed upon the screen.

32